Spirits Rising

White Loon
85

The Native Tutoring Centre and Frontier College
would like to acknowledge the Ministry of Citizenship and Culture
for the Government of Ontario for making the publication of Spirits Rising possible.

Spirits Rising

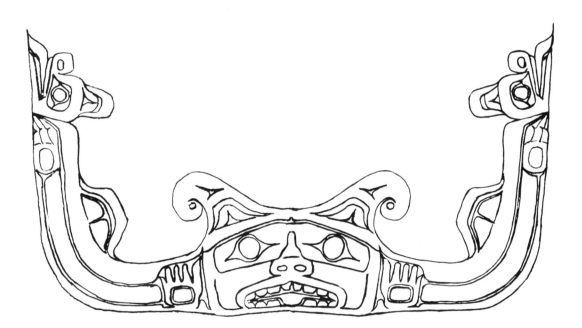

Written by Native Indian People
from different nations
attending the Native Tutoring Centre in British Columbia.
Published by Frontier College Press, Toronto, Ontario.

Written by the students attending the Native Tutoring Centre, Vancouver, British Columbia

Canadian Cataloguing in Publication Data

SPIRITS RISING

ISBN 0-921031-03-3

1. Canadian literature (*English*) – 20th century.*
2. Canadian literature (*English*) – Indian authors.*
I. Frontier College.

PS8235.I5S65 1986   C810'.8'0897   C86-093881-6
PR9194.5.I5S65 1986

Designed and Produced by
THE CLELAND COMMUNICATIONS GROUP INC.

Published by
FRONTIER COLLEGE PRESS
35 Jackes Avenue
Toronto, Ontario
M4T 1E2

Contents

Preface 6
Introduction 7
Friday Night by Dan Howard 9
The New Home and the Old Home by Betty Gladue 10
My Home Town by Russell Wilson 13
Dear Ken Loo by Gloria Christopher 17
Matthew by Leonard Prince 18
All In A Days Work by Philip Gladue 21
Unfinished Pipe by Ken Loo 25
My Friend by Joe Walkus 27
Hugs by Linda Innes 29
When I Used to Play Hockey by Mark Wilson 31
Dear Lorraine by Eddie Chartrand 33
People by Robin Ringland 35
Murray's Christmas Holidays by Buddy Hill 37
I Had A Dream by Erica Cynthia Martin 39
Bike Riding Around Stanley Park by Sam Innes 40

Because the emphasis of our program is on the spirit of writing, rather than adhering to conventional spelling and syntax, the writings in this book have been reproduced accurately, without editorial intervention.

Preface

The stories and letters found in this book have been illustrated by Mike WhiteLoon – an Ojibway Indian artist from Manitoulin Island in Ontario. Mike now resides in Vancouver with his wife, Dianne, and their young daughter, Rosanne.

Mike often donates his artwork to native organizations for fundraising purposes. He has spent much of his life travelling across Canada and the United States, talking to people in universities about Indian culture. Informally, Mike has demonstrated his feelings and insights into his culture through such events as the Peace March from Sacramento to Washington in the 1970s.

We hope Mike's illustrations in this book will contribute to furthering a greater awareness of native Indian culture.

Some of the illustrations have been provided by Duane Howard, a member of the Mowachaht Band, a small band on the west coast of Vancouver Island.

Special thanks to both our artists for capturing the spirit of the writers' thoughts.

To those people who gave ideas and inner thoughts to this book and its readers, our gratitude. Your strength has been shared by all of us.

And for your efforts: Linda, Phil, Betty, Ken, Danny, Russell, Gloria, Robin, Leonard, Sam, Mark, Joe, Eddie, Duane and Mike – we are proud!

At the time this book was put together, the Tutoring Centre was a program supported by a special partnership between two groups – The Urban Native Indian Education Society and Frontier College. These two groups were represented by a partnership in the co-ordination – Jack Gundaker and Joni MacArthur. Thank you for your support that helped make this book possible.

Our logo is the Sisiutle, a legendary, two-headed creature of the West Coast Indians that was able to change itself into whatever it chose. This is our symbol for the relationship between tutor and student – a relationship with the potential of transforming both participants into something very different. This logo, originally carved in cedar, was contributed by Blaise Chartrand.

We hope you will enjoy reading this book as much as we have enjoyed bringing it together.

Introduction

SPIRITS RISING is more than just a book of extraordinary art and powerful writing by people who were told they could not write. **SPIRITS RISING** is what can happen when partnerships evolve around issues that are important to people's lives.

Frontier College has been creating and supporting programs to help adults read and write since 1899. We have long been aware of the dilemma facing urban Natives. We decided to try an experiment and so formed a partnership with the Native Education Centre in Vancouver and created the Native Tutoring Centre.

It worked. Students learned and wrote and graduated into the Centre's programs. Since publishing student writing is such a powerful motivator, we began gathering writing and then art from the Vancouver program. It took on a momentum of its own.

Time passed, and not for lack of material, but for lack of money was the publication of this book delayed. And now, thanks to the generosity of the Ministry of Citizenship and Culture of the Government of Ontario, the book is here.

We think that this book is very special and will help to create new possibilities for Native and non-Native students from coast to coast. In images and words it carries a powerful message about the future we can have if we build partnerships that support people. It is a statement about what can be.

From all of us who have been involved in the production of this book, we hope it will be as inspirational for you to read as it was for the people who wrote and illustrated this very special book.

Jack Pearpoint
President, Frontier College

White Loon
85

Friday Night

Dan Howard

*D*anny Howard comes from Gold River, Vancouver Island, B.C. He's a member of the Mowachaht Band. He's 20 years old and finally getting back into writing again. Danny is a newcomer to the tutoring center but will probably be writing a lot more.

*N*ovember 20th, 1985

Friday night again but Brian didn't know what to do cause he just came to town. It was his first time in years he had been in Vancouver. His family kept on warning him about the big cities. The big cities made him feel stronger, at least that's what he thought.

Brian knew some people in town that said he could phone any time he was there, so he gave them a call but it was too late, nobody was home. So he decided to go to town to look for those people. He caught the first bus he saw and didn't know where he was going. There was a place he had heard about a lot, he just passed so he got off and walked about two blocks and he saw some people getting beat up by a gang. He didn't know what to do so he panicked and started to help those guys that were getting beat up. As soon as he got involved, he found himself sitting in back of a police car.

He wasn't able to explain himself because he was being smart to the cops. So he spent his time in jail while he was in Vancouver. When he got home his family asked how his trip was. He didn't want to tell anything to them but he realized what they were trying to tell him before he left. So he told them and said he is not going to go and do something he's not sure about.

The New Home and the Old Home 1970

Betty Gladue

Betty Gladue, 37 years old, was born in Moberly Lake, B.C. She is presently working on regaining her status as a member of the Saulteau Band. She has recently joined the upgrading class at the Native Education Centre. In her words, when asked how things were going, she says, "She's flying".

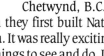he place where I came from is Chetwynd, B.C. I lived there when they first built Native housing in Canada. It was really exciting, with a lot of new things to see and do. It was a new way of living in a new home. There were 32 new houses built there. When we saw homes being built, lots of families were happy. How excited we were to live in a new home! There were new things to learn how to operate in the house. We learned how to light the furnace and how to pay bills. It was scary when we had a lot of responsibility. It was scary for the people that were going to live there because I heard these people talking about it, and I was one of them.

When I first cooked bannock it didn't turn out because I didn't turn the timer on the stove. But it was lots of laughing and thinking of new ways of cooking. Other people that lived there didn't sleep because the furnace was too loud. It kept them awake because the furnace was too noisy. Also, my husband was a handy man there. He understands some things that work in the home. But one day he said it was getting hard to understand about things. But it was a learning experience he had with people in their homes. He had a lot of laughing and joking about things that were hard to understand.

The children that grew up in their new homes were happy. There were many new things for them to see. One thing I noticed the children weren't getting sick anymore. Also, many kids finished school there and some went to university to get their degree. I am very proud of them. Someone still in high school. It's nice to see many new things happening in their lives.

I lived in the old home before they built the new housing. We used to call the place where we lived Moccasin Flats where the Natives lived for a long time. It was my grandfather's and grandmother's land. Squatters were allowed to live there for three hundred dollars, just as long as they kept the land clean. They could grow vegetables if they wanted. But grandpa didn't give the Squatter's the land title.

One day my grandma took sick. She had stomach cancer, so my grandfather sold the land to someone in Vancouver. He didn't tell the Natives living their because it would hurt their feelings. I heard grandpa talking about the man who bought the land who sold it to the town of Chetwynd. Then they had to do something to the Natives. So they formed a committee that had Native people and town involvement.

They had to do something to move them because they were building a big airport somewhere there. And the committee knew that there was some crown land available. They sold it to Natives for one dollar per lot. There were many volunteers that were helping build houses. They started to build 32 homes in Chetwynd. That's when CMHC got involved to build houses for Natives. They started to build homes for low income people.

But the old home had good memories. Because there was a lot of hard work to be done, like hauling water, chopping wood, hunting game, keeping garden and getting up in the morning to make fire. No one was lazy in those days. One thing you didn't have to pay bills because you had to work for it.

12

HOWARD/85

My Home Town

Russell Wilson

I'm a 41 year old native of Kispiox, B.C. The Gitksan Carrier is the name of my band. Since June 1985, I've worked on researching and writing about my culture. My main interest is the history behind totem poles. I now attend the Native Education Centre in the Native Adult Basic Education class of the NEC.

This summer was the first time that I ever went home within about twenty-five years. Home is up north at Kispiox, B.C. I finally made the decision to go home one way or the other; I was going and I made it. For a long time during those years I've been dreaming and wanting to go home. So all these years past, and just the thought of being home was really thrilling and exciting, for awhile. The only welcome home I got was from my own family and the rest was all a flunk.

The first day I arrived in Hazelton, in the morning at 5:00 a.m., I had to take a taxi home to Kispiox. It cost me $23.00, and my family threw a big party. That morning and for three whole days we partied, and it turned out really succesful, but the greatest welcome home coming that I enjoyed was from all my nieces and, my nephew when they were calling me uncle everyday, right to the last day till I left. It was also the first time I've met my sister's husband. They've been married for a least thirty years and she now has four daughters and one son. All my nieces and nephew really treated me quite well, and I was really getting a kick out of them. Every morning they were cooking breakfast for me, taking turns and bringing me coffee plus dinner too. And

now I'm beginning to miss them all cause I used to play a lot of card games with them and go for long walks, but mainly I am missing my nephew because we sure used to go fishing together a lot and bike riding and shared the bedroom and discussed a lot of things together.

Now, about my fishing trip: like I said, from the beginning, it's the first time I've ever been home in twenty-five years. On the first day the first fish I landed was the hump-back, and about a week later I caught a jack spring plus the biggest spring salmon that weighed sixty-three pounds and it took me two and a half hours to land it. I was really excited and scared at the same time of loosing that big fish. Wow! What a fish!. About two weeks later I was the one who caught the first coho salmon. It wasn't the biggest, but it must have weighed about fourteen pounds, and, believe it or not, I almost forgot what coho looked like, and all the other fishes too. I also caught the biggest steel head, which weighed approximately eighty pounds roughly, but it got away. I also caught quite a lot of dolly bardins and rainbow trout. They were all good sizes, about eight to ten pounders.

I just bought a hundred and fifty yards of line; it was a twenty-five pound test and that darn steel head took off with the

(continued next page)

whole line. It almost pulled me in too. Well, you guys you can just imagine what kind of summer holidays I had up north in Kispiox, B.C. I saw plenty of black bears, moose, beavers, otters, deers, ducks etc, (even though I wasn't hunting for them). They were lucky I wasn't. All I could do was watch them, but what they don't know was what was going on in my mind, that I was really envying them because they have got all the freedom in the world, that they can go and travel all over across the country with nothing to worry about and they have lots of nutrition out there to live on, especially those wild birds and the eagles, I sometimes envy them the most because they can fly right across the country with nothing too much to worry about and they're free as ever can be.

I was always picking a few variety of berries, for example, huckleberries, raspberries, gooseberries, cranberries, blueberries, blackberries, saskatoonberries, and wild soupberries. I don't know if you have ever heard of these kinds of berries but you can make Indian ice cream out of them and they're delicious and juicy. "Wow"! What a dish!!

Feelings, however, I am not exactly sure where I stand among my people anymore. So I called friends and the people that I once knew I don't know where they went to or what happened to them or myself. So during those five weeks I was there, I felt for the first time in my entire life that I ever felt so deeply resented among my own people. All the time I was there all they could say was, "Hello". How are you? "Or how have you been doing?" And the "Good-bye". I felt like a total stranger with no face. Perhaps most of them are married with families too, and some probably think they're not good enough or too good or I'm not good enough for them anymore, or perhaps they think that I am too civilized for them. I just don't know anymore than they do, because my feelings are absolutely mixed-up.

Dear Ken Loo

Gloria Christopher

Hi, my name is Gloria Christopher. I'm from Canim Lake reserve. I went to school in three different areas. I wanted to go to school in town because they put me in a special Grade. When I finish at the tutoring centre here I'd like to be a secretary or a House wife.

October 17/85

Hi, how are you doing? I hope that you are doing all right, because I think you are all right in my book. I think that you are a fine looking guy. I like working with you. Some day I will know you and your wife better and I will always write to you. I will be thinking of you a lot more because I will be going home may be February, I don't really know I will be very sad if I go home because I will be missing all my friends. I will always keep you in my memories.

I was going to ask you if you wanted a beaded necklace for your self. I really want to make you one if you want one. I really admire you alot. I want to be your friend as long as we live.

One more thing I want to tell you is that people up there on the reserve do alot drumming because they want to know alot about our culture and spiritual things. Spit in the water or the fire, then some thing will happen to you and hurt you alot. People will pray in the tent. You have to be in a circle to ask the great spirit to help you. You have to tell him that you need his help and that you need help talking with others about your problems. The other people will be listening to you. Tell them that you are having a lot of problems in your life and you get it off your chest and out of your mind.

That's what I had to do. I have alot and I was so scared because I had to face other people to tell them about my problems I couldn't face anyone at all until I learned some of my culture. I know a little bit but I still have to learn more about my culture and I want to know all about the people that lived a long time ago because I was never born. They never had a bar or a store I don't really about long time ago. One other thing I was practicing on was my Indian dancing. I know that you got to practice on it really really lots and you will get the hang of it.

Yours truly

Matthew

Leonard Prince

Leonard Prince comes from Fort St. James, B.C. and has been around for 30 years. He loves children so much that he and his wife, June, are guardians for their neice and nephew, Matthew and Georgia. He now attends the Native Education Centre.

I remember when Matthew first came into our life. He was shy. It took him a few days before he would say anything to us on his own. Matthew would walk around like he was unsure what was going to happen next. When I told him that June and I really loved him and his sister, he gave me that kind of look that should he believe me or was I just saying that to make him feel better.

I see a lot of me in Matthew; he is really cautious, and has a very good memory. When I saw him after four years I could see all the hurt and pain on his face. I remember that one day I walked up behind him, he turned real fast and looked real scared; he asked me what was I going to do. I replied nothing honey! I was watching you playing with the doggie. I asked him if I could hold him and he said why? I said because I love you Matthew and that I missed him, he told me his mommy doesn't say that to him.

Since he has lived with June and I, he has begun to open up and is not so shy, he loves playing hide and seek, walking on the beach, going to Stanley Park, loves Kentucky fried chicken, also fresh fruit (plums) and he is starting to let other people into his life. He likes his friend Jack and asks when is he coming to visit him.

Matthew has changed a lot and he and his sister have brought a lot of happiness into our lives and I am only sorry we couldn't have come into his life sooner. Because he and his sister don't deserve that kind of life, so it is up to us adults to change our kids lives and make it better so that when they have children they wouldn't be treated like that. So please help me make it a life to live and not a life to want to die before they have had a chance to live! Amen.

July 4, 1985

Howard/85

20

All In A Days Work

Philip Gladue

For me, my wife and daughter, breaking out of the rural environment and living in a fast urban city, is a wonderful and exciting experience.

Going back to school after twenty-seven years is a superb feeling, meeting new friends, doing new things, knowing that you are part of this society that we live in.

I've worked twenty-seven years in heavy construction, as well as falling trees in logging camps and various labour jobs.

I found in the last three years, construction and logging job opportunities were getting scarce. My family and I decided to up-grade our education for future goals.

I am amazed how this Tutoring Centre has helped us to keep our native culture alive and adapt to urban society. I am really thankful for opportunities found in the city and help from native centres.

I am writing about one of my hunting trips in the North east of British Columbia, not too far from Dawson Creek, B.C. Every year in the fall, I hunt moose for our meat supply.

I usually go to an area, where there are salt licks. In this trip my wife and two daughters were with me. We headed out for Pine Pass right at the foot of the mountains. After driving for two hours, I parked the car. The plan was for them to wait in the car for me, while I checked the salt lick for signs of moose, half mile away.

Walking for about ten minutes closer to the salt lick, I noticed a lot of fresh game tracks, mostly moose, a few deer, and bear.

The wind was blowing in the right direction for me. I knew I could get real close. There were game trails coming from all directions into the lick.

I decided to stop and listen for a while. Standing and listening for about ten minutes, I could hear squirrels dropping cones off the trees, birds singing, chattering, and a warm wind blowing softly through the spruce and pine trees.

Then all of a sudden I heard the crack of a stick, right away I, loaded my gun real slow, so as not to make noise.

Standing still and bracing myself against a pine tree, I could hear light pounding of hooves on the ground.

So I stood real still until I could see a black figure in an opening. I could see a small cow moose coming towards the salt lick, I didn't move because I knew there be a bull moose around shortly.

I watched the small cow go down to lick the salt off the mud.

Watched her for at least five minutes before hearing a grunt from the far end of the opening. I lifted my gun and pointing it towards the south, I could see a large set of horns heading towards the cow. The bull moose was moving fairly fast.

I got pretty excited! I didn't want to make a mistake, lucky enough the bull stopped right close to the cow.

So I quickly aimed for the neck and pulled the trigger, down went the bull moose. The cow moose ran off slowly into the brush. I walked right up to the dying moose, taking out my knife to cut it's throat and letting it bleed from the neck. I knew my work had just begun.

The moose was an average size and dark colour. I knew it was fat, because most of the dark bulls are fat at that time of year!

I tried to turn it over on it's back but couldn't; it was too heavy. The only thing for me to do was open the stomach and go back to the car for help. When I got to the car. The kids asked what I was shooting at and if I'd killed anything.

(continued next page)

21

Betty my wife asked if the moose was fat because she had good hunch I shot at a moose. I said it's a good size. I've come for your help. We'll have to take the kids with us They all agreed and were excited. So we started back, it took about twenty minutes to get there. The kids were five and six years old. I had to pack the youngest one, Debbie, over windfall and second growth.

Betty and Sandra our oldest daughter were having a hard time keeping up.

When we got to the kill, I said to them, "have a good rest before we start skinning."

While we were resting, I sharpened my knife. It was getting late in the afternoon and we had a lot of work to do. I figured it would take at least two more hours before we could head back.

Betty and I rolled the moose on its back so I could gut it out. We didn't have too much of a problem; Betty is pretty strong. After gutting the moose out, I had the kids hold one of the front legs while skinning it. Debbie the youngest, said she would pack the leg they were holding and right a way Sandra, the oldest said to her mother that she would pack the other. The sun was setting fast by the time I got finished skinning and quartering the meat, I said to Betty and the kids, "we better start back; it'll be dark by the time we get to the car." As we started back the kids asked if, they could pack a front leg each. Jokingly, I said "tomorrow would be a better time", they agreed with a smile.

It was late by the time we got the car. Tired and hungry we drove home.

White
Loon
85

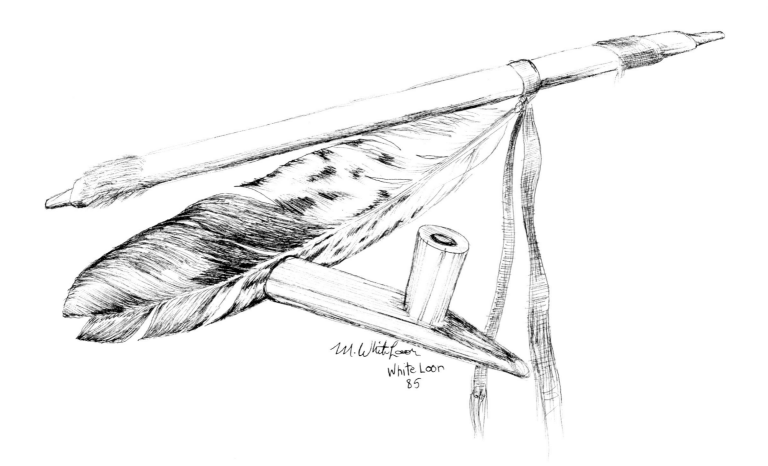

Friday Night

Dan Howard

Danny Howard comes from Gold River, Vancouver Island, B.C. He's a member of the Mowachaht Band. He's 20 years old and finally getting back into writing again. Danny is a newcomer to the tutoring center but will probably be writing a lot more.

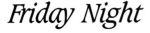

ovember 20th, 1985

Friday night again but Brian didn't know what to do cause he just came to town. It was his first time in years he had been in Vancouver. His family kept on warning him about the big cities. The big cities made him feel stronger, at least that's what he thought.

Brian knew some people in town that said he could phone any time he was there, so he gave them a call but it was too late, nobody was home. So he decided to go to town to look for those people. He caught the first bus he saw and didn't know where he was going. There was a place he had heard about a lot, he just passed so he got off and walked about two blocks and he saw some people getting beat up by a gang. He didn't know what to do so he panicked and started to help those guys that were getting beat up. As soon as he got involved, he found himself sitting in back of a police car.

He wasn't able to explain himself because he was being smart to the cops. So he spent his time in jail while he was in Vancouver. When he got home his family asked how his trip was. He didn't want to tell anything to them but he realized what they were trying to tell him before he left. So he told them and said he is not going to go and do something he's not sure about.

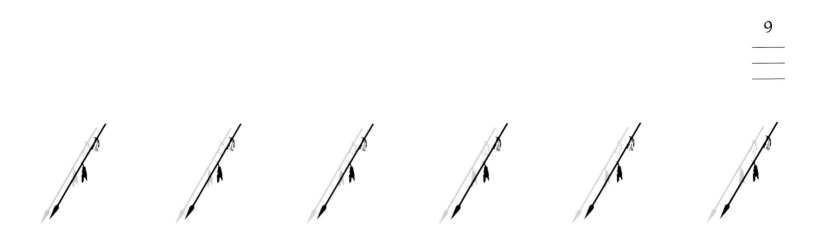

The New Home and the Old Home 1970

Betty Gladue

Betty Gladue, 37 years old, was born in Moberly Lake, B.C. She is presently working on regaining her status as a member of the Saulteau Band. She has recently joined the upgrading class at the Native Education Centre. In her words, when asked how things were going, she says, "She's flying".

*T*he place where I came from is Chetwynd, B.C. I lived there when they first built Native housing in Canada. It was really exciting, with a lot of new things to see and do. It was a new way of living in a new home. There were 32 new houses built there. When we saw homes being built, lots of families were happy. How excited we were to live in a new home! There were new things to learn how to operate in the house. We learned how to light the furnace and how to pay bills. It was scary when we had alot of responsibility. It was scary for the people that were going to live there because I heard these people talking about it, and I was one of them.

When I first cooked bannock it didn't turn out because I didn't turn the timer on the stove. But it was lots of laughing and thinking of new ways of cooking. Other people that lived there didn't sleep because the furnace was too loud. It kept them awake because the furnace was too noisy. Also, my husband was a handy man there. He understands some things that work in the home. But one day he said it was getting hard to understand about things. But it was a learning experience he had with people in their homes. He had a lot of laughing and joking about things that were hard to understand.

The children that grew up in their new homes were happy. There were many new things for them to see. One thing I noticed the children weren't getting sick anymore. Also, many kids finished school there and some went to university to get their degree. I am very proud of them. Someone still in high school. It's nice to see many new things happening in their lives.

I lived in the old home before they built the new housing. We used to call the place where we lived Moccasin Flats where the Natives lived for a long time. It was my grandfather's and grandmother's land. Squatters were allowed to live there for three hundred dollars, just as long as they kept the land clean. They could grow vegetables if they wanted. But grandpa didn't give the Squatter's the land title.

One day my grandma took sick. She had stomach cancer, so my grandfather sold the land to someone in Vancouver. He didn't tell the Natives living their because it would hurt their feelings. I heard grandpa talking about the man who bought the land who sold it to the town of Chetwynd. Then they had to do something to the Natives. So they formed a committee that had Native people and town involvement.

They had to do something to move them because they were building a big airport somewhere there. And the committee knew that there was some crown land available. They sold it to Natives for one dollar per lot. There were many volunteers that were helping build houses. They started to build 32 homes in Chetwynd. That's when CMHC got involved to build houses for Natives. They started to build homes for low income people.

But the old home had good memories. Because there was a lot of hard work to be done, like hauling water, chopping wood, hunting game, keeping garden and getting up in the morning to make fire. No one was lazy in those days. One thing you didn't have to pay bills because you had to work for it.

11

CHOWARD/85

My Home Town

Russell Wilson

I'm a 41 year old native of Kispiox, B.C. The Gitksan-Carrier is the name of my band. Since June 1985, I've worked on researching and writing about my culture. My main interest is the history behind totem poles. I now attend the Native Education Centre in the Native Adult Basic Education class of the NEC.

This summer was the first time that I ever went home within about twenty-five years. Home is up north at Kispiox, B.C. I finally made the decision to go home one way or the other; I was going and I made it. For a long time during those years I've been dreaming and wanting to go home. So all these years past, and just the thought of being home was really thrilling and exciting, for awhile. The only welcome home I got was from my own family and the rest was all a flunk.

The first day I arrived in Hazelton, in the morning at 5:00 a.m., I had to take a taxi home to Kispiox. It cost me $23.00, and my family threw a big party. That morning and for three whole days we partied, and it turned out really succesful, but the greatest welcome home coming that I enjoyed was from all my nieces and, my nephew when they were calling me uncle everyday, right to the last day till I left. It was also the first time I've met my sister's husband. They've been married for a least thirty years and she now has four daughters and one son. All my nieces and nephew really treated me quite well, and I was really getting a kick out of them. Every morning they were cooking breakfast for me, taking turns and bringing me coffee plus dinner too. And

now I'm beginning to miss them all cause I used to play a lot of card games with them and go for long walks, but mainly I am missing my nephew because we sure used to go fishing together a lot and bike riding and shared the bedroom and discussed a lot of things together.

Now, about my fishing trip: like I said, from the beginning, it's the first time I've ever been home in twenty-five years. On the first day the first fish I landed was the hump-back, and about a week later I caught a jack spring plus the biggest spring salmon that weighed sixty-three pounds and it took me two and a half hours to land it. I was really excited and scared at the same time of loosing that big fish. Wow! What a fish!. About two weeks later I was the one who caught the first coho salmon. It wasn't the biggest, but it must have weighed about fourteen pounds, and, believe it or not, I almost forgot what coho looked like, and all the other fishes too. I also caught the biggest steel head, which weighed approximately eighty pounds roughly, but it got away. I also caught quite a lot of dolly bardins and rainbow trout. They were all good sizes, about eight to ten pounders.

I just bought a hundred and fifty yards of line; it was a twenty-five pound test and that darn steel head took off with the

(continued next page)

13

whole line. It almost pulled me in too. Well, you guys you can just imagine what kind of summer holidays I had up north in Kispiox, B.C. I saw plenty of black bears, moose, beavers, otters, deers, ducks etc, (even though I wasn't hunting for them). They were lucky I wasn't. All I could do was watch them, but what they don't know was what was going on in my mind, that I was really envying them because they have got all the freedom in the world, that they can go and travel all over across the country with nothing to worry about and they have lots of nutrition out there to live on, especially those wild birds and the eagles, I sometimes envy them the most because they can fly right across the country with nothing too much to worry about and they're free as ever can be.

I was always picking a few variety of berries, for example, huckleberries, raspberries, gooseberries, cranberries, blueberries, blackberries, saskatoonberries, and wild soupberries. I don't know if you have ever heard of these kinds of berries but you can make Indian ice cream out of them and they're delicious and juicy. "Wow"! What a dish!!

Feelings, however, I am not exactly sure where I stand among my people anymore. So I called friends and the people that I once knew I don't know where they went to or what happened to them or myself. So during those five weeks I was there, I felt for the first time in my entire life that I ever felt so deeply resented among my own people. All the time I was there all they could say was, "Hello". How are you? "Or how have you been doing?" And the "Good-bye". I felt like a total stranger with no face. Perhaps most of them are married with families too, and some probably think they're not good enough or too good or I'm not good enough for them anymore, or perhaps they think that I am too civilized for them. I just don't know anymore than they do, because my feelings are absolutely mixed-up.

Dear Ken Loo

Gloria Christopher

Hi, my name is Gloria Christopher. I'm from Canim Lake reserve. I went to school in three different areas. I wanted to go to school in town because they put me in a special Grade. When I finish at the tutoring centre here I'd like to be a secretary or a House wife.

October 17/85

Hi, how are you doing? I hope that you are doing all right, because I think you are all right in my book. I think that you are a fine looking guy. I like working with you. Some day I will know you and your wife better and I will always write to you. I will be thinking of you a lot more because I will be going home may be February, I don't really know I will be very sad if I go home because I will be missing all my friends. I will always keep you in my memories.

I was going to ask you if you wanted a beaded necklace for your self. I really want to make you one if you want one. I really admire you alot. I want to be your friend as long as we live.

One more thing I want to tell you is that people up there on the reserve do alot drumming because they want to know alot about our culture and spiritual things. Spit in the water or the fire, then some thing will happen to you and hurt you alot. People will pray in the tent. You have to be in a circle to ask the great spirit to help you. You have to tell him that you need his help and that you need help talking with others about your problems. The other people will be listening to you. Tell them that you are having a lot of problems in your life and you get it off your chest and out of your mind.

That's what I had to do. I have alot and I was so scared because I had to face other people to tell them about my problems I couldn't face anyone at all until I learned some of my culture. I know a little bit but I still have to learn more about my culture and I want to know all about the people that lived a long time ago because I was never born. They never had a bar or a store I don't really about long time ago. One other thing I was practicing on was my Indian dancing. I know that you got to practice on it really really lots and you will get the hang of it.

Yours truly

Matthew

Leonard Prince

Leonard Prince comes from Fort St. James, B.C. and has been around for 30 years. He loves children so much that he and his wife, June, are guardians for their neice and nephew, Matthew and Georgia. He now attends the Native Education Centre.

I remember when Matthew first came into our life. He was shy. It took him a few days before he would say anything to us on his own. Matthew would walk around like he was unsure what was going to happen next. When I told him that June and I really loved him and his sister, he gave me that kind of look that should he believe me or was I just saying that to make him feel better.

I see a lot of me in Matthew; he is really cautious, and has a very good memory. When I saw him after four years I could see all the hurt and pain on his face. I remember that one day I walked up behind him, he turned real fast and looked real scared; he asked me what was I going to do. I replied nothing honey! I was watching you playing with the doggie. I asked him if I could hold him and he said why? I said because I love you Matthew and that I missed him, he told me his mommy doesn't say that to him.

Since he has lived with June and I, he has begun to open up and is not so shy, he loves playing hide and seek, walking on the beach, going to Stanley Park, loves Kentucky fried chicken, also fresh fruit (plums) and he is starting to let other people into his life. He likes his friend Jack and asks when is he coming to visit him.

Matthew has changed a lot and he and his sister have brought a lot of happiness into our lives and I am only sorry we couldn't have come into his life sooner. Because he and his sister don't deserve that kind of life, so it is up to us adults to change our kids lives and make it better so that when they have children they wouldn't be treated like that. So please help me make it a life to live and not a life to want to die before they have had a chance to live! Amen.

July 4, 1985

Howard/85

Spirits Rising

All In A Days Work

Philip Gladue

For me, my wife and daughter, breaking out of the rural environment and living in a fast urban city, is a wonderful and exciting experience.

Going back to school after twenty-seven years is a superb feeling, meeting new friends, doing new things, knowing that you are part of this society that we live in.

I've worked twenty-seven years in heavy construction, as well as falling trees in logging camps and various labour jobs.

I found in the last three years, construction and logging job opportunities were getting scarce. My family and I decided to up-grade our education for future goals.

I am amazed how this Tutoring Centre has helped us to keep our native culture alive and adapt to urban society. I am really thankful for opportunities found in the city and help from native centres.

I am writing about one of my hunting trips in the North east of British Columbia, not too far from Dawson Creek, B.C. Every year in the fall, I hunt moose for our meat supply.

I usually go to an area, where there are salt licks. In this trip my wife and two daughters were with me. We headed out for Pine Pass right at the foot of the mountains. After driving for two hours, I parked the car. The plan was for them to wait in the car for me, while I checked the salt lick for signs of moose, half mile away.

Walking for about ten minutes closer to the salt lick, I noticed a lot of fresh game tracks, mostly moose, a few deer, and bear.

The wind was blowing in the right direction for me. I knew I could get real close. There were game trails coming from all directions into the lick.

I decided to stop and listen for a while. Standing and listening for about ten minutes, I could hear squirrels dropping cones off the trees, birds singing, chattering, and a warm wind blowing softly through the spruce and pine trees.

Then all of a sudden I heard the crack of a stick, right away I, loaded my gun real slow, so as not to make noise.

Standing still and bracing myself against a pine tree, I could hear light pounding of hooves on the ground.

So I stood real still until I could see a black figure in an opening. I could see a small cow moose coming towards the salt lick, I didn't move because I knew there be a bull moose around shortly.

I watched the small cow go down to lick the salt off the mud.

Watched her for at least five minutes before hearing a grunt from the far end of the opening. I lifted my gun and pointing it towards the south, I could see a large set of horns heading towards the cow. The bull moose was moving fairly fast.

I got pretty excited! I didn't want to make a mistake, lucky enough the bull stopped right close to the cow.

So I quickly aimed for the neck and pulled the trigger, down went the bull moose. The cow moose ran off slowly into the brush. I walked right up to the dying moose, taking out my knife to cut it's throat and letting it bleed from the neck. I knew my work had just begun.

The moose was an average size and dark colour. I knew it was fat, because most of the dark bulls are fat at that time of year!

I tried to turn it over on it's back but couldn't; it was too heavy. The only thing for me to do was open the stomach and go back to the car for help. When I got to the car. The kids asked what I was shooting at and if I'd killed anything.

(continued next page)

Betty my wife asked if the moose was fat because she had good hunch I shot at a moose. I said it's a good size. I've come for your help. We'll have to take the kids with us They all agreed and were excited. So we started back, it took about twenty minutes to get there. The kids were five and six years old. I had to pack the youngest one, Debbie, over windfall and second growth.

Betty and Sandra our oldest daughter were having a hard time keeping up.

When we got to the kill, I said to them, "have a good rest before we start skinning."

While we were resting, I sharpened my knife. It was getting late in the afternoon and we had a lot of work to do. I figured it would take at least two more hours before we could head back.

Betty and I rolled the moose on its back so I could gut it out. We didn't have too much of a problem; Betty is pretty strong. After gutting the moose out, I had the kids hold one of the front legs while skinning it. Debbie the youngest, said she would pack the leg they were holding and right a way Sandra, the oldest said to her mother that she would pack the other. The sun was setting fast by the time I got finished skinning and quartering the meat, I said to Betty and the kids, "we better start back; it'll be dark by the time we get to the car." As we started back the kids asked if, they could pack a front leg each. Jokingly, I said "tomorrow would be a better time", they agreed with a smile.

It was late by the time we got the car. Tired and hungry we drove home.

White
Loon
85

23

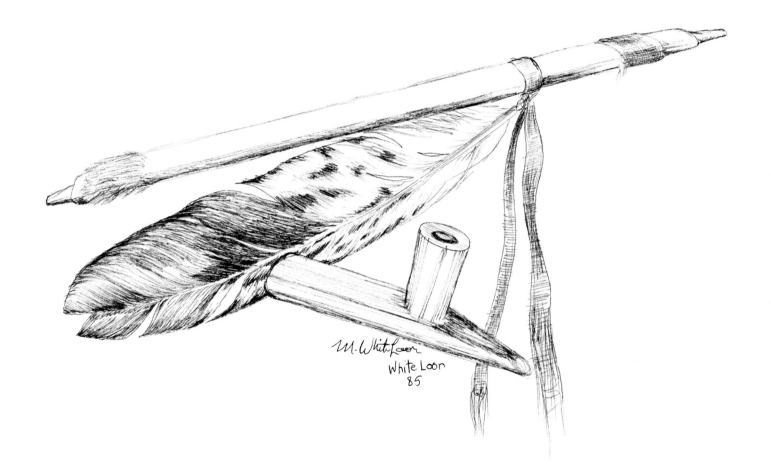